Sell more with sales letters

How to write targeted sales letters and convince your customers - incl. checklist

Carsten Meinders

All advice in this book has been carefully considered and checked. Nevertheless, no guarantee can be given. Any liability of the author or the publisher for any personal injury, property damage or financial loss is therefore excluded.

All rights reserved, in particular the right to reproduce and distribute the translation. No part of this work may be reproduced in any form (by photocopy, microfilm or any other process) or stored, processed, duplicated or distributed using electronic systems without the written permission of the publisher.

CONTENT

Foreword 1

Chapter 1 - Introduction 3

All about a sales letter 3

Comparison between unsolicited proposals, brochures and sales letters 6

Segmentation, targeting and positioning 9

The AIDA model 11

Chapter 2 - Basic elements of a sales letter 16

What are the basic components of a sales letter? 16

The image 1

Headline job 1

Welcome and introductory paragraph 1

Letter content 2

Conclusion or call to action 3

One last suggestion 3

How do you create headlines to energize your sales letters? 4

Seven surefire headlines 4

Is it important to have a strong first paragraph? 6

Is a P.S. essential in your sales letter? 8

Should you include warranties? 10

Seven tips for a great guarantee 11

Chapter 3 - Tips for writing a sales letter........... 14

Basic tips for writing an effective sales letter 14

A 12-step guide to writing a good sales letter16

What basic questions should your sales letter answer? 25

Are aesthetics important for your sales letter? 27

Tips on how to make a sales letter look good: 28

Do short, powerful sentences improve the impact of your sales letter?.............................30

Why certain sales letters are poorly received.34

What are fatal flaws in sales letters?...............38

What are the pitfalls of a "what if" approach? 41

What to do if you just can't write a sales letter? 43

The difference between a sales letter and an advertisement 46

Attention is crucial 47

A quick lesson in writing sales letters in a clear manner 49

Which is better - a long or a short sales letter?
.... 52

Do you always have to use correct German? 54

A monster of a sales letter 55

Is it true that good sales letters are like good
salespeople ? 60

The ten basic rules for writing a good sales
letter 63

Five useful secrets of an effective sales letter 66

Do emotionally charged sales letters increase
sales? 68

What words you should never use in a sales
letter 72

Ways to build reputation 75

Chapter 4 - Completion of the work 77

Final checklist for a sales letter 77

Closing words 80

Foreword

Dhe fundamental goal of any business is to increase the value of the operation to shareholders. Whether you want to get a big response to a newspaper or magazine ad, a direct sales letter, or a website, you need to be aware of the following basic fact:

"What is it that makes your company special?" An important and frequently used marketing communications tool is the sales letter. It can build your customer base and increase your sales.

What's so special about sales letters that are always read? What's so special about sales letters that sell products? What is the secret of sales letters that readers read to the last line? Why do we buy based on some sales letters and not others, even though they offer the same benefits and features?

Anyone can write a wonderful sales letter. Sure, you may need to learn some new skills. But today's famous copywriters weren't born knowing how to write good sales letters.

They all started from scratch. They also had their initial difficulties and failures. But they persevered. Once you know how to play the game, you'll find for yourself that writing an effective sales letter is a piece of cake.

This e-book takes you step-by-step through the process of writing an effective sales letter, from what your goal is, to the basic elements of a sales letter, to valuable tips on how to improve your sales letter to increase sales ... You will find it all in this e-book.

Enjoy reading.

Chapter 1 - Introduction

ALL ABOUT A SALES LETTER

A sales letter is a document designed to promote sales. It is intended to persuade the reader to place an order or request information about a product or service. The basic goal is to motivate the reader to take a certain action.

Results of my research and development

"I am turning to you to let you know about the really great washing machine that I have developed. First of all, I know it is wonderful because I have spent years working on washing machines of all kinds. Then I expanded my field of research and development (R&D) to include all kinds of commercial washing machines, and I've been privy to all kinds of secrets that make sure dirt comes out in the most unimaginable places. Now, TEN YEARS LATER, I am ready to let you enjoy the fruits of my hard work. I have developed the EZ WASHER. I have to tell you that it will put all other washing machines you have ever seen to shame."

Do you find anything wrong with this sales letter? Almost everything is wrong.

The headline is only about the author and not about the customer. Also, some technical terms are used - "R&D" for research and development. This is an industry term that might irritate some potential customers. We have no idea what the 10 years of work refers to. Nor are we given any unusual features. The author just generally gushes about what a great job he has done. The sales letter talks about all that he has done in the last 10 years, not what I will get, or at least what I can expect.

Before you start writing a sales letter, you need to try,

Put yourself in the position of the potential customer. Be clear about how you handle unsolicited letters you receive. Most of these letters, if not all, go into the trash. Some you don't even open. That's why I've first briefly summarized below the most important reasons why you should create a sales letter.

a) It draws attention to the product and services you offer

The primary and most important reason for using sales letters as a marketing tool is to make the customer aware of your product or service by engaging the reader with appropriate facts.

b) Find an excuse for a future appointment

The sales letter can be used to make the consumer aware of future contact, for example, by visiting them in person or calling them for an appointment.

c) Answering inquiries

If the customer has asked for additional information about a particular product or service at an earlier stage, a sales letter can be sent to respond to their questions. This in itself may be a basis for selling the product or service.

d) General information

A sales letter can inform the consumer about the latest offers, products, services, sales, and so on. It may be any other information that you believe will interest the reader. The consumer may have specifically asked you to inform them of such information and/or you may be targeting consumer groups exclusively.

To figure out how you should write your cover letter, it is important to define your goals. If you are clear about your goal, it will be easy for you to apply the necessary technique. Here are some of them:

COMPARISON BETWEEN UNSOLICITED PROPOSALS, BROCHURES AND SALES LETTERS

Whether you are preparing a brochure or writing an unsolicited proposal, you can always do better by recognizing the similarities and differences between them.

A brochure is a document about your products and services. It is often produced on a large scale and distributed incognito. Brochures come in different shapes and sizes and are usually printed in bright colors and with many graphics.

An unsolicited offer is an article about your products and services. It is usually created independently and given to a specific person (even if it is someone you don't know too well). It often takes the form of a letter, unless it is a large document that is bound.

A sales letter is a short offer and is always aimed at getting you to take a certain action. Depending on the situation, sales letters may or may not be addressed to specific people, and sometimes they are sent to people you do not know.

So what is the dissimilarity? It turns out that in reality there is not much difference between them. All of them need to provide information and usually try to influence. Sometimes the main goal of a brochure is to provide information. A key differentiator is whether the brochure aims to get you to take a particular action. Marketing materials are almost always designed to encourage the reader to do something. That might be a visit to the store, a purchase, a visit to a website, or perhaps just a phone call. If your brochure simply delivers information, you should rethink it to make sure it's compelling and consider redesigning it to move people to action.

If you have a call to action, or something that you want the

inspire potential customers, then it can be helpful to think of your brochure as an unsolicited proposal. The brochure should be designed to effectively persuade the reader to carry out the call to action.

When writing a sales letter, you may not understand that it is not much different from a brochure that calls the reader to action. Try to focus on the aesthetics of the brochure.

With both brochures and unsolicited offers, there is a danger of not having enough information about the reader. The more you know about the reader, the more persuasive you can be. However, brochures and unsolicited offers are often given to people you don't know too well, usually with the expectation of getting to know them better.

The next time you create a brochure, unsolicited proposal, or sales letter, take the time to think about it as if it were one of the other documents. Use the comparison to improve the document, but be clear about your goals and audience.

SEGMENTATION, TARGETING AND POSITIONING

When preparing your sales letter, you really need to know the product or service being offered, the market dynamics, and the reader's stated and unstated needs. There is no substitute for product or service knowledge.
What does the product or service do for the person who needs it? How can the reader benefit from the purchase? What is the unique selling proposition of the product or service? To answer these questions, you should first distinguish the benefits from the features. The sales letter should be able to convince the reader to buy your products based on the benefits the product/service offers, not on its features.

A benefit is what the product or service offers and how the consumer benefits from the feature. A benefit is the specific result of the feature. A feature is what the product or service already has built in. The benefit is what encourages people to buy. For example, a refrigerator has a defrosting device (feature). If this technology helps get rid of unwanted icicles and keeps our vegetables fresh and healthy, then we have the benefit of this feature.

Decide how you want to advertise the product or service. Through the Internet, direct mail, email, direct sales, print advertising, etc.? Is there other advertising or literature that supports the cover letter? Who is your competition? What marketing activities have they undertaken? What is your advertising budget? Are your goals too high?

Who is your potential buyer? What inspires a person to buy that item? Experts point out that the most common emotion used to get people to buy is fear, and a million other variations of it. You need to put yourself in the consumer's shoes to see if your offer appeals to their emotional needs.

THE AIDA MODEL

Copywriters follow the AIDA model. The AIDA model stands for
Attention, interest, desire (in English, "Desire"), and action or action.

**Attract the attention
of your readers**

If you want your sales letter to resonate with your readers, you must first grab their attention. You can do this with a hard-hitting headline or introductory paragraph that hits the nail right on the head, or you can even start your letter with a compelling question. For example, "Would you like to cut your electricity costs by 45%?"

An appropriate headline for a promotional letter for a weight loss program might read, "Now you can lose 15 pounds in 2 weeks without starving yourself; and it's easy and affordable!" This headline not only solves a problem, but also provides a quick and easy solution that keeps the price-sensitive consumer in mind.

Your reader will only be interested in knowing the following: What's in it for me? Why should I invest my time to read on? If you tell him this at the very beginning of your letter, he will continue reading the rest of the letter, and that's already half the battle won. In any case, he will rarely reach the third paragraph. So the effect must be immediate. The heart of the matter should be explained right at the beginning.

Arouse interest

You need to capture the reader's interest by showing them why they need your product or service. You must create a need for your product or service. Let him know how his life will be easier with your product. Show him what he is missing out on if he doesn't even try the product. This is where you need to demonstrate your trustworthiness. You can support your arguments with testimonials or case studies. You can provide the communication details of users who have benefited from your product. Always remember that you know everything about your product, so "stale news" will seem like "fresh news" to you.

Arouse desire

Now you have gained the reader's attention and piqued their interest. Next, you need to create desire. Tell the reader how exactly they will benefit from your product. Link the benefits to the reader's daily life. Make him realize how your product will benefit him, how convenient it will be for him to get it, and how pleasant life will be for him afterwards.

Generalities are less convincing. Specific details are much more believable. For example, if you want to sell books on reducing employee theft, "By the end of this quarter, your employee theft rate could drop by more than 37%. Imagine the spectacular effect this will have on your bottom line!" Or if you're selling a weight loss program, "Within 3 weeks you will have lost 7 kilograms. Imagine the compliments you will receive from your spouse. Imagine how stunning you will look in your new swimsuit!"

Call to action

What should the reader do next? Send in a reply card? Order the product or service? Call and ask for more information? Make an appointment? Inform him accordingly. It's amazing how many sales letters fail to inform the reader of the next step. They assume that the reader is a mind reader. But that is usually not the case.

Until now, you have worked hard. You have attracted his attention, aroused his interest, awakened desires. Isn't it appropriate to call for action? Don't assume your reader knows what to do next. To support the desired action, always include a response card with your letter.

The P.S. is a component of a letter that is always read. Use the P.S. to highlight your most compelling advantage or to reinforce your guarantee. Don't waste it on amusement. Used judiciously, it could be the final push that tips the buying decision in your favor. So be specific and give the final push.

Chapter 2 - Basic elements of a sales letter

WHAT ARE THE BASIC COMPONENTS OF A SALES LETTER?

Each sales letter follows roughly the following sequence:

a. Image

b. Headline

c. Greeting.

d. Main paragraph

e. Body

f. Close

The image

If there is a logo or design for your company, only use it in your cover letter if it is truly relevant to what you offer. You are not selling your company logo, you are selling the benefits the buyer will have when they purchase your product or service. Use a specific image that matches your headline, content, and topic, or don't use an image at all. Stick to words as much as possible.

Headline job

The headline is usually 3 to 30 words long. It should be catchy. It should catch the reader's attention and tell him what the ad (sales letter) is about. Ideally, the headline has the task of arousing the reader's concentration, appealing to the viewer, mentioning a benefit and making an assurance.

Welcome and introductory paragraph

Any sales letter that influences the reader has a chance to be opened and read.

o Spin a thread that the reader can identify with, using a conversational tone.

o Announce a new product or service, an exclusive event or important news, highlighting your unique selling proposition.
o Address the reader at eye level: "Dear car buyer, do you know that ..."
o You could start with something new, perhaps a quote or an anecdote.
o You could start by identifying the reader's problem that your product promises to solve.
o Ask a question that might excite the reader.
o Point out a mystery or unusual information to the reader.

You could use a subheading to answer a question posed in the headline. For example, Part A might read, "Would you like to lose 7 pounds in 3 weeks at an affordable price?" Part 2 might read, "Well, here's how you can do it ..."

Letter content
The main text should have the same tone and pick up on the theme of the headline. You should continue to highlight the benefits and cite evidence to support your claim. Provide details about the benefits and features. Build

credibility. Your basic goal is to create a need for your products or services and get people to do what you want them to do.

Conclusion or call to action

If you are asking the reader to order something, to support you, or to contact you, you must make it easy for them to respond. You must provide the sales letter with a stamped return envelope and an order form. If this is not possible, include a toll-free phone number, an email link, and/or your URL. Always thank the reader for their patience. Always use a postscript.

One last suggestion

The real challenge is to get the reader to spend their hard earned money on you. The best way to do this is to use test readers. Test readers can give their opinion on whether something is missing from the letter.

HOW DO YOU CREATE HEADLINES TO ENERGIZE YOUR SALES LETTERS?

Each of your marketing tools needs a headline. Headlines grab attention, make your message easy to read, get to the heart of your key selling points, and get your customers to buy the product or service.

Use regular headlines in your sales letters to help readers understand your main message without having to dig around too much.

Headlines range from "punch in the face" to more subtle ones that don't seem like headlines at all.

Your headline will be noticed if it appeals to the reader's interests. You need to use your headline to refer to a difficulty the reader has or something you know the reader feels strongly about.

Seven surefire headlines

a. **Ask a question**. "Are you afraid of getting fat and flabby?" A question in the headline forces an answer in the reader's mind. You mechanically engage the potential customer in your message.

b. **Start your headline with "How to"**. "How to lose 7 pounds in 3 weeks." People love information that shows how to do something valuable.

c. **Provide a testimonial**. The advice of a satisfied customer can act as a catalyst to get others to buy from you.

d. **Give a command**. Some traditional headlines ask readers to "aim high," "get ahead," etc. Turn your key advantage into a strong headline.

e. **Significant news makes a good headline**. This works especially well when there are big changes in your company or new product launches.

f. **Give a final date for a special offer**. Most of us are always too busy and tend to put off taking action. "Save money now" and "Get a bonus if you buy now" increase response.

g. **Free offers often get the biggest response**. There is a myth that wealthy or professional clients are put off by free offers. This is not true at all. Simply tailor your free offer to the style of your clients or your industry.

Prospective customers are always under time pressure. They are inundated with hundreds of ads, sales letters, postcards and commercials every day. They tend to tune out any advertising message that seems like it will take a long time to understand. Headlines help them decide. So focus on them.

IS IT IMPORTANT TO HAVE A STRONG FIRST PARAGRAPH?

The next crucial question is how to start your cover letter.

Do you immediately tell the potential customer what you want to sell him? Do you touch him just a little so he understands why he needs your product or service?

The course of the first paragraph of your sales letter depends on the topic you have chosen. This theme will determine whether your introductory paragraph takes a particular creative approach or focuses on your offer.

Once your first paragraph is in line with your theme, the focus should be on the warm-up phase. An ineffective warm-up phase cripples a sales letter more than any other aspect and results in an average letter.

A good sales text gets right to the point. Your goal is to capture the reader's interest. The point is not to lay the groundwork for understanding the text, but to create immediate interest in your chosen topic.

Also, the first paragraph should be written in the first person. A quick way to make a letter unreadable is to speak in the third person or to insert "we" into the letter. Starting a letter with "we" can spoil your response.

Here is a comprehensive list of rules to follow when writing your first paragraph:
a. Make it theatrical, interesting, and right on target for the audience.
b. Keep your paragraph short.
c. Keep your sentences precise.
d. Keep your words short.
e. Use the word "you" to address the potential customer.
f. Have your message come from a single person, on a very individual basis, with the goal of building a one-to-one readership throughout the post.

g. When evaluating a sales letter, check the introductory paragraph first and foremost. Does it match the approach and flavor of the six points above?

There is no rigid formula for an introductory paragraph, but your letters will elicit better responses if you stick to the rules instead of breaking them.

IS A P.S. ESSENTIAL IN YOUR SALES LETTER?

People want to know who sent them the letter and tend to quickly scroll to the end of the letter to see whose signature is at the bottom.

The next thing they see below the signature is a postscript (or P.S.). In fact, your P.S. may be the second (after the headline) or third (after the introductory sentence/paragraph) most-read element of your sales letter or email. Most copywriters use not only one postscript, but several (P.P.S.).

Most postscripts are relatively short, usually about 3 or 4 lines, summarizing the offer, confirming the deadline, and including the call to action.

The Duden defines P.S. as follows (literally):

"Postscript - Postscript; a paragraph added to a letter after it has been completed and signed by the writer; an addition added to a letter or composition after the main body of the work has been completed, containing something omitted or something new that occurs to the writer."

For marketers, it provides a final opportunity to move potential customers to action. The best way to use the final "addendum" is to highlight or repeat an important point that matters to the reader.

Apply these tactics. The P.S. is one of the most read elements of any sales letter. It ranks second only to the headline and subheadings when it comes to readership priority.

Be brief and to the point. A concise summary is enough to keep the reader interested. If you need more space, insert a second P.S. Adding additional P.S. is an effective strategy, especially for longer sales letters.

SHOULD YOU INCLUDE WAR-RANTIES?

If you offer a product or service without a war-ranty, you could be about to lose a large per-centage of potential sales. Nowadays, scams are widespread. Since there are no official police or moderators on the Internet, the number of scams is probably even greater.

Because of these scammers and the large num-ber of challenges online, people are suspicious and increasingly looking for more protected means to profit from offers. Guarantees are therefore an influential tool for the opulent marketer and can do two very important things that help increase their own profits: increase sales and reduce returns.

When you offer a guarantee, you reduce distrust around the purchase of your product or service. Consumers are pretty cautious, and even more so when they buy over the Internet. And warranties give you an almost instant trustworthiness with potential customers.

Guarantees increase the perceived value. Take, for example, the story of the Monaghan brothers.

Both brothers worked in a home office. They needed money to pay for college. They worked shifts and attended college when they had the other shift off. After losing money for about a year, one of the brothers sold his share of the business. The other stayed in the small pizzeria. In some recent interviews, Tom Monaghan said he wasn't sure he was doing the right thing. And the rest is history. His decision was the best he ever made. His business was based on a simple guarantee - "Fresh pizza in 30 minutes or free" - and Domino's Pizza became the billion-dollar industry it is today.

Warranties increase sales and reduce returns.

Return chicanery increases expediency and gives the buyer more confidence. So use guarantees to ensure your success.

Seven tips for a great guarantee
o Make the warranty simple and straightforward. Ditch the excuses and the fine print.
o Make sure your entire company is confident in the operating philosophy set forth by the use of warranties.

o Be familiar enough with your customers to know if the warranty will help the customer at all.

o A guarantee should be reciprocal, meaning that if you exceed your performance potential, you should charge a contingency fee.

o Specify which customers are eligible for the warranty and which are not. Limit the number to a minimum.

o Respond quickly when a customer asks you to honor your warranty.

o Monitor your performance to avoid surprises.

The guarantees can be divided into five very different categories:

o The money back guarantee: It guarantees that your customers will not waste their time or money. It also protects the customers if the product breaks or fails.

o The satisfaction guarantee: it guarantees that your customer will be happy and satisfied with your service or product.

o Price guarantee: This can be either a fixed price that ensures that the price and/or payment terms will not change or increase (e.g., life insurance), or a guarantee that the customer will not find a lower price elsewhere.

o Punctuality guarantee: This helps to quell the fears of customers who are under time pressure. For companies such as printers, car repair shops and cable companies, such an offer can be tempting.

o Absolutely No-Questions-Asked Guarantee: This can be applied to anything. Just try it and see.

Chapter 3 - Tips for writing a sales letter

BASIC TIPS FOR WRITING AN EFFECTIVE SALES LETTER

a. **Build credibility**. In addition to mentioning the benefits, you should also include testimonials from people who have already used and benefited from your product or service. This increases credibility.

b. **Make it memorable for your reader**. Most unsolicited mail ends up in the trash can. Your mailer should contain something unique to make people take more time to read it. For example, a car repair service might include the 10 best tips for car maintenance and so on.

c. **Emphasize the aesthetics**. The letter should be user-friendly. It should have an attractive visual impact. The aesthetic should be well defined. It should also be easy to navigate.

d. **Include a call to action**. Include a postcard, stamped envelope, and/or order form. If not appropriate, include a toll-free phone number, email link, and/or your URL.

e. **Always use an incentive**. The letter should include an incentive for quick action - a discount, special offer, gifts, etc.

f. **Resist the "mail merge" function.** Technology has undoubtedly made life easier. But try not to write mass letters. Personalize each letter according to the reader's needs.

g. **Establish lasting relationships**. Try to build lasting relationships with your customers. To do this, you need to "under-promise" and "over-deliver".

h. **Test the market**. Whatever technique you want to use, always test the market.

i. **Strike the right tone**. Your sales letter should not be too formal and full of technical terms. This could put off the reader.

j. **One last tip**: before sending out the mailings, make sure you have calculated all aspects. You certainly don't want to be flooded with offers without having the appropriate funds.

A 12-STEP GUIDE TO WRITING A GOOD SALES LETTER

You don't have to be an award-winning copywriter to write competent sales letters. In fact, writing great sales letters is more of a science than an art. Even professionals use proven "templates" to create sales letters that get the results they want.

Everyone has some form of buying resistance. The basic goal of your sales letter should be to overcome your reader's resistance to purchase and move them to action. These hurdles make themselves felt in many stated and unexplained customer comments, such as:

"They don't recognize my real problem."

"How do I know you're competent?"

"I don't believe you at all."

"I don't need it right now."

"It's not going to help me in any way."

"What happens if I don't find it useful?"
"I can't afford to buy it."
etc.

The sales letter must appeal to the reader's emotions to the point where they are prompted to act. The letter should try to appeal to the "hot buttons" or emotional pressure points that make the reader want to buy. The two most important motivators are the prospect of profit and the fear of loss.

Would you rather buy a $60 course on "How to advance your career" or "How to avoid getting laid off"?

Every day the second title will sell better. And why? Because it addresses the fear of loss.

Below is a 12-step model for writing foolproof sales letters.

Try to attract attention:
Assuming the reader has opened your envelope, the next important step is to grab their attention. The headline is the most important thing your reader pays attention to. People have a very limited attention span and usually

throw their mail in the trash unless the headline catches their eye.

Below are three examples of headline templates that are proven to keep you focused.
INSTRUCTION _______________________
THE   ESSENTIAL   SECRETS   OF
_______________________ENTHÜLLT!
WARNING: DO NOT VENTURE _________
BEFORE VISITING ________________.

Identify the reader's problem: Now that the reader has given you their full attention, you need to directly address the problem area. Try to put yourself in the reader's shoes.

Another method is to trigger the problem. You portray the problem and dramatize it so that the person really feels the pain and anguish of their situation. Humans are such robust creatures of habit that they rarely bother to change their habits unless they feel great pain. Indeed, companies are not diverse. Most companies keep doing the same thing until it gets so bad that they have to change something.

Offer the solution to the problem: After identifying the reader's problem, you become the "savior" by offering him the solution to the problem. You introduce your product or service and show him how all his problems will disappear once he gets your product/service.

Present your qualifications to the prospect: If you just tell the reader that you can make their life more comfortable and convenient, they won't be swayed to buy your products. You need to build trust and prove your credibility. You can do this in the following ways:

o Listing of successful case studies and examples

o Name reputable companies (or individuals) with whom you have done business

o Mention of your work experience

o Show important awards and prizes you have won

Point out the benefits of your products: Now you need to tell the reader how they will personally benefit from your product or service. Don't just mention the features. No one is interested only in the features. What you can do instead is draw two columns. In one column you can write the features and in the other you can write all the conceivable benefits that the reader can get from the feature. You can also use bullet points for each benefit to make navigation user-friendly.

Give your social proof: now that you have presented all your advantages, you need to strengthen your credibility and your readers' trust with testimonials from satisfied customers.

Testimonials are influential sales tools that prove your claims are true. Another way to make your testimonial even more influential is to include pictures of your customers with their names, addresses and phone numbers. Most readers won't call to find out. But if you include the numbers, it gives you more credibility.

Make your final offer: Your offer is the most important element of your sales letter. If your offer is great, it will be irresistible even with mediocre sales copy.

Your offer can be designed in many different ways. The best offers are usually an attractive mix of price, terms, and free additions. It is always more lucrative to enhance your offer with more and more

benefits than just lowering the price.

Make a promise or guarantee: You can make your offer even more attractive by taking the risk factor out of it. Remember that people have a built-in fear that marketers want to scam them.

Give a very strong guarantee, but only if you have enough confidence in your product or service. If you give a guarantee and later fail to live up to it, your credibility is shattered. So be careful. If your product or service is good enough, very few people will actually need a refund.

Bring in the elements of scarcity: Most people take a long time to respond to offers, even when they are tempting. There can be many reasons for this, for example:
o They don't feel enough discomfort to change anything.

o They are too busy and eventually forget.
o They do not believe that the perceived value justifies the asking price.
o They are just lazy.

To get people to act, you need to add incentives to the supply. You can create a sense of scarcity by informing the reader that either the offer or the quantity is limited. You can also mention that your offer is only valid for a limited time.

Your offer might go something like this:
"If you shop by (date), you'll get a whole bunch of freebies."
"Our supply is limited to 60 pieces (product or service) and you will receive them on a 'first come, first served' basis. When they are used up, there are no more available."
"This price is only valid for the next 15 days."

But once you make such an offer, you can't undo it and keep extending the last date. This will make your customers lose trust in you.

Call to action: Don't assume that your reader knows what to do to enjoy your offer. You need to carefully guide him on how to place the order in very understandable and concise language. Tell him whether he should call you, send you a fax, or click the order button on your website.

Issue a warning:

A good sales letter should evoke emotion even after the call to action.

You can use the "risk of loss" strategy to let the reader know what would happen if they don't use your existing offer. Example:

Fight forever:

o Lose the chance to get all your valuable goodies.

o No improvement in life.

o See how your competitors benefit and move up in life.

Try to give the reader a sad picture of the punishment that awaits him if he doesn't take action now. Make him realize how much he is missing out on right now.

Close with an appropriate reminder

You should always include a postscript (P.S.). In this postscript, you can remind your customers of your enticing offer. If you talked about scarcity in your sales letter, include your call to action and then remind them of the limited time (or quantity) offer.

With this 12-step formula, anyone can write an effective and sales-boosting cover letter. Below are some additional tips to help you write an even better sales letter:

Tip 1: Always mention the features/benefits - The biggest obstacle to writing a brilliant sales letter is to start simple. Take a pen and paper and list all the features of your product or service. Then take another piece of paper and list the benefits that can be derived from your product or service.

Tip 2: When you are done with the letter, forget about it for a day or two.
This will allow you to be more practical when editing your letter.

Tip 3: Create a "scrapbook" to boost your creativity. When you see a well-crafted ad or sales letter on a website, or receive a really effective letter in the mail or email, keep it in a file or folder that you can refer back to again and again. Keep comparing ideas.

Tip 4: Create a customer profile before writing your sales letter .
Use a sheet on which you record everything you know about your target customer.

Tip 5: Keep your cover letter as long as it needs to be. You can make it a short 2-page article or a 50-page e-book. The essential purpose of both is to stir emotions and call to action.

WHAT BASIC QUESTIONS SHOULD YOUR SALES LETTER ANSWER?

Who are your potential customers?
Before you write your sales letter, you need to target your customer group. You should know who you want to sell your product or service to. If you were offering a golf club designed for golfing, you wouldn't market it to men in general. You would tailor it to the people who play golf. You have to be very specific.

How is your product or service different from others?

How does your product differ from the competition? Have you done a comparative study? If there is something unique about your product, show it to the readers.

Why should the interested party have faith
have?

With all the scams and fake information spread in advertising, skepticism sets in very quickly. So you need to make sure that your prospect believes what you are telling them to be the incontrovertible truth. Build your credibility by offering statistics and testimonials.

What are the benefits that your product or service offers the consumer?

List all the visible and not so visible benefits that make your product irresistible.

Why might your prospect reject your offer?

Put yourself in the position of your prospective buyer. That way, you know what reservations or objections he might have. Once you know them, work on them and resolve the issues.

Why should your prospect act now?
The final question you need to answer for your prospect is why he needs to act without further ado. Give him a real reason to act immediately. Make him a special price if he acts within the next few days. Or tell him that quantities are limited and that once inventory is depleted, you won't sell at the same price. Just make sure y-our call is credible.

ARE AESTHETICS IMPORTANT FOR YOUR SALES LETTER?

Is appearance important to you? Like most pe-ople - including your customers and prospects - your answer is yes. Especially in sales, appearance is critical. In a competitive situa-tion, for example, all other things being equal, the appearance of the salesperson can be the deciding factor in who closes the deal.

Appearance is also crucial to the success of your sales letter.

The marketer with a very targeted mailing list, a strong offer and a successful text - and the one who pays attention to how his letter looks - will definitely receive more offers than the one who only focuses on the content without paying attention to the aesthetics. The more memorable it is, the better.

Tips on how to make a sales letter look good:
Tip 1: Always use a reader-friendly font. Almost all newspapers and news magazines use mostly serif fonts for their editorial content. Fonts like Times New Roman, Courier, and Century are far more readable than fonts like Arial or Helvetica.

Tip 2: Make your headline catchy. Also, keep your introductory paragraph to one to three lines.

Tip 3: Try to limit the length of all paragraphs to 4 to 6 lines. Your letter should have an inviting, reader-friendly look. Your prospect will

certainly not be thrilled to see clumsy paragraphs with 9 to 11 sentences.

Tip 4: Vary the length of your heels so they
don't get too boring.

Tip 5: Set the text of your writing in 10-11
point and use subheadings, bullets, and other
devices to grab attention. Always keep in mind
the audience you are writing for. If you are writing for the target audience of 20-somethings,
you can most likely even use 10-point font. On
the other hand, if you are targeting the "adult"
market, you should use 14-point font. Centered,
highlighted subtitles and other attention-grabbing elements can increase readership.

Subheadings, bulleted lists, highlighting,
and other devices add appeal to your writing
and increase response. However, be careful to
use these devices carefully. Overuse can negate
their overall effect.

If you take these 5 tips to heart, you'll attract more eyeballs, ensure longer reading time,
generate more leads, and ultimately close more
sales.

Always remember that your letter is competing with perhaps dozens of other sales letters you receive every day, sent by vendors vying for attention. To stand out from this clutter, your cover letter must be excellent, diverse, competent and relevant.

DO SHORT, POWERFUL SENTENCES IMPROVE THE IMPACT OF YOUR SALES LETTER?

A slogan is a "noun, usually repetitive and persuasive, that is a catchy phrase, motto, or jingle that expresses a specific goal or concept. A concept that is intended to be imprinted in the minds of the audience like glue on paper."

What makes a slogan memorable? The first aspect to consider is conciseness - usually 10 words or less. The slogan should follow a certain rhythm.

Second, what are the advantages of using slogans? As mentioned earlier, brevity meets the demands of today's fast-paced world. Slogans also manipulate decisions, persuade and build trust. A slogan usually makes it easier for a prospect to remember and identify a product or service.

Simple, powerful phrases motivate your customers' feelings and create an emotional decision to buy from you. You can increase your sales by using powerful phrases in your sales letters.

Strong wording helps your customer imagine how they will feel when they own your product or use your service. It creates an imaginary feeling and motivates your customer to turn that feeling into reality. Powerful wording increases the customer's desire for your product or service and leads to an emotional purchase decision.

Creating a power phrase is simple. Start by recording some of the key benefits your customers will receive when they choose to buy from you. Then add some punchy action words related to one or more of those benefits to create a short phrase.

Below are some examples of power phrases used by different types of companies:
"Quick! Simple! Affordable!"
"I assure you that you will get immediate results with my product."

Pay attention to the words used in the two expletives above. Expletives use effective words to make forceful statements.

The most effective power phrases usually combine 3 words or 3 groups of words in a row. Take for example:
"Save time. Save money. Save trouble."
"Quick! Simple! Affordable!"
"Enjoy it at home, in the office or in the car."
"Authority, Power and Momentum!"

There are five main types of slogans:
o **A characteristic**: a peculiarity or difference between a substance, product, or object. Example: "Write an e-book in 10 days."
o **A benefit**: a result that someone receives. "Think of it as saving [time or money]."
o **One question:** food for thought. "How would you like to make money without having to invest a single penny?"
o **A challenge**: a test of courage. Example: The Marines - "We're just looking for a few exceptional men."
o **A structure**: a design that can be assembled for a specific purpose.

There are seven ways to make a slogan memorable:

o Make it exciting
o Being arrogant
o Self-Reference
o Figurative, playful or humorous
o Inspiring or motivating
o Create painful memories
o Use of dramatic language

Life slogans help reinforce goals and dreams and even change beliefs. In business, slogans are typically used for self-promotion, presentations, websites, email signatures, and even speeches. Come up with something, use a slogan in each of your sales and marketing processes, and change it regularly as needed.

Where do you start to develop slogans? Read through all your notes or materials. Emphasize phrases that contain a lot of energy. Rhymes help create excellent slogans. Read poetry to find clues or language that influence or inspire you.

WHY CERTAIN SALES LETTERS ARE POORLY RECEIVED

Any consultant can tell you that there are numerous ways to lose a sale even when you are sure you will win it. Most often, the loophole is in the sales letter itself. Most salespeople drool when customers ask for quotes. After all, it's exciting to present your products to a potential customer, convince them, and then close the deal. But it's not that easy to create an impressive offer, and the process takes a lot of time and energy.

Below are some of the reasons why a sales letter loses sales and how to avoid it.

1. Do not play the lonely caretaker

Some do thorough research on the client and the project and think that's more than enough. Then they sit down and create their proposal in isolation. This is a serious mistake. You can't just create a proposal unless the customer is actively involved in every stage of the proposal process, including research, goals, potential benefits, scope, approach, and so on.

2. Do not start with your qualifications

Don't start your offer with your company's great story. Your customers are interested in what you can actually do for them. Start your first paragraph with the program, not how great you are.

3. Do not neglect the Executive Synopsis

Many decision makers are bothered by two things in particular: the summary and the price. Yet it's surprising that some salespeople don't include summaries in their sales letters. Decision makers rely on the summary to make sure you understand what they are trying to accomplish. If you leave out the summary, you can be sure your letter will end up in the trash.

4. Don't just focus on your tools

Customers are only interested in the result, not the tools, methods and approaches you use to achieve the result. Don't talk about how you're going to do this and that. Tell them what you can do and how quickly. The "how" can be discussed later when you have landed the project.

5. Short and sweet

Research shows that when given a choice, customers are more likely to consider a shorter proposal than to get lost in a long, windy sales letter crammed with graphics and standard wording. Keep your proposals as short as possible, but make sure you meet your customers' needs.

6. Do not use the same resume

Each situation is different from the other in some way. So you cannot present the same resume to everyone. Prepare different templates. Customize your resume for each client. Let the clients know what different experiences you have.

7. Do not overload your offer with Jargon

Most sales letters are full of jargon and technical-sounding words. Such flowery language may be suitable for textbooks, but it usually puts off the customer. Try to use simple and informative language.

8. Do not cut and paste

To save time, some companies believe in the cut-and-paste syndrome. And what is the result? The customer receives one company's offer with another's name and address, or vice versa. Go over the cover letter thoroughly before you send it to the customer or post it on your website. Save yourself the embarrassment.

9. Be on time

Don't try to bluff your customers. If you missed the deadline for submitting the sales proposal, be honest and ask for an extension. Do not try to make nonsensical excuses.

A brilliant proposal can be crucial to winning a project; a bad proposal can cause you to blow it, even if other things in the sales process went perfectly. So try to avoid the basic mistakes mentioned above.

WHAT ARE FATAL FLAWS IN SALES LETTERS?

If you want to be successful, the prospect must open, read, believe and respond to your sales letter. To achieve this, it must generate interest and create a desire for your product or service. A successful sales letter should achieve the same result as a successful salesperson. Similar to a salesperson, the sales letter will also want to avoid certain mistakes.

Here are a few deadly mistakes most sales letters make.

Lethal Sales Letter Mistake #1 - Don't try to use bulk mailers. You are sending your sales letter in bulk. But the recipient will not appreciate this fact. The moment he sees that it is one of those bulk mails, he will delete it.

If you compose your writing with a "herd mentality" rather than focusing on a single, individual prospect, it hurts the chance that your writing will make a real connection with the reader.

A sales letter is the only marketing tool that works from person to person. So make it as personal as possible.

Deadly mistake #2 - Don't write long, boring letters. In your opinion, what is a long letter? Even a one-page letter can seem long. This is because it is not the length that is long, but the content of the letter.

People watch long movies, read long books, and so on. But only if they are interesting. If you get bored over and over again, there's a good chance you'll end up in the nearest trash can.

Offer a suitable product or service at a reasonable price and present it in an interesting way. Half the battle is won.

Deadly Mistake #3 - Don't just stick to grammatically correct, formal German. In school, your teachers and professors were paid to correct your work according to the formal rules of grammar. But in the real world, it's a whole different ball game.

You should write your letter in "common" and informal language to make it more user-friendly. You may need to violate certain grammar rules. You may need to begin sentences with "and" or "but." You may have to use abbreviations and word fragments. The main goal of a sales letter is not to get a grade of 1, but to generate sales.

Deadly mistake #4: Don't allow the reader to make an excuse for not reading your writing. In reality, no one cares who you are or what product or service you offer. They are only interested in how they can benefit from you.

So you need to grab attention in the first 20 seconds or even less. Start with a provocative sentence or slogan. Try to appeal to the emotions. Your goal should be to grab the potential customer's attention.

Deadly sales letter mistake #5: You don't properly present your credentials.

The evidence you cite in your cover letter to support your pedigree can take many different forms. For example:

Include testimonials from people who have used and benefited from your product or service. Include them in the form of stories. To make your testimonials even more powerful, include pictures of your customers with their names, addresses and phone numbers. Most readers won't call to find out. But if you include the numbers, it gives you more credibility.

WHAT ARE THE PITFALLS OF A "WHAT IF" APPROACH?

"How about if I could show you how to save money even though you're not reducing your daily expenses?"
"What if I told you that you could increase your market share in three months?"
"How about I have you lose weight in no time?"

But what if you are a potential consumer who has heard these "false" statements before? Do you think you'll even have enough motivation to buy then?

Schematic sales practices are rarely successful when it comes to dealing with customer resistance, and they really have no place in the world of competent selling.

The real method is to remove your potential customers' resistance during the sales process. This means asking the right questions early on and customizing your product or service so that it solves the problem.

It is true that many people will object to buying your products. The best way out of this situation is to inquire about their real needs, try to gauge their problems, and offer them a product or service that will actually benefit them. And for that, you need to spend a lot of time with them.

You need to ask top-notch questions that make your customer think. This may sound very simple, but it's actually very complicated because challenging questions are hard to ask. Many salespeople consider these types of questions personal and often assume that their customers won't be excited to answer them.

It is important to remember that most people ask difficult questions and consequently have little or no uncertainty in answering them. On the contrary, it will improve your position in their eyes.

You can ask questions like:

o What are your short-term goals?

o How do you intend to achieve these goals?

o What difficulties do you encounter in achieving these goals?

Your basic goal in this conversation is to find out what problem the prospect has and how you and your product or service can solve it.

Let's not run away from the truth. Buyers today are much more complicated than ever before and most likely they have already heard everything you want to say. And they detest people who use clichéd and traditional phrases or manipulative approaches.

Most people express certain objections regarding a purchase decision. For example, sales occur because your customer recognizes the value of your product or service, or because you have proven to be a specialist who can help them solve a problem.

The question "What if I could" is not a successful advance. It's a cliché and hardly works these days.

WHAT TO DO IF YOU JUST CAN'T WRITE A SALES LETTER?

You want to write a sales letter, but you just can't find the right words. You think and think and think, but to no avail. What do you do now?

This is a really annoying situation and can happen to all of us at any time. But there is a great way to get the creative juices flowing.

Ask questions

Do you really know your product?

Let's say you're selling a treadmill. You really need to know how it feels to use it. When can you use it? What are the limitations and side effects?

When you know and appreciate your product, you feel the need to tell the whole world about it. To praise it. To love it. To show it off.

With this, the first hurdle has been overcome. Now that you know the product and have fallen in love with it, you can describe it.

Then note the reasons why and how it will help you, if at all. Will it make my life easier? Will it add value? Will it solve a problem? Also, is it too expensive? Is it too ugly? And so on.

List everything: the good, the bad, and even the ugly.

You need to find out the reason why people will buy from you in the first place.

What is so unique about your product or service? The best way to do this is to brainstorm.

Soon you'll have so many opinions flooding in that you won't be able to keep up.

Just continue the process until you've exhausted all the ideas.

When you're done with that, all you have to do is look at your notes and make a list of all the spectacular ideas you have. List them in order of priority.

Now you have the draft for your letter.

Use the most important base on the list, the main motive why someone should buy your product, and turn it into a wonderful headline.

Incorporate the ideas on the list into your cover letter and use subheadings or highlighting when you want to emphasize a point. Soon your letter will have almost written itself.

When writing your letter, remember to write it to one person at a time. Make it special!

THE DIFFERENCE BETWEEN A SALES LETTER AND AN ADVERTISEMENT

The terms advertisement and sales letter are often confused. Both are used to attract new customers or sell a product or service. But there are significant differences in the way they work.

A sales letter is a more individual form of advertising than any advertisement. An ad in a magazine or newspaper is seen by thousands or even millions of readers. A sales letter is for the reader's eyes only. Even though sales letters are often printed in large quantities, the reader perceives the mail as more personal than an ad in a newspaper or magazine.

Unlike an advertisement, a sales letter is more personal, informal and cordial. This conveys a casual and natural tone. In this way, the reader gets a better sense of the writer's character, interest, and seriousness.

ATTENTION IS CRUCIAL

For any marketer, attention is a precious commodity. With consumers bombarded with thousands of direct mail pieces every day, the challenge of how to make your message stand out from the crowd becomes even greater.

Every successful sales letter must accomplish two things:

1. He must get the prospect to read the entire letter.

2. He must get the prospect to perform the desired action.

If the marketer has not achieved step 1, step 2 is impossible.

Many marketers try to make the envelope very attractive. They know that their battle is half won if they can get the prospect to open the letter.

For online marketers, there is no prospect of an envelope. Some webmasters create Flash images to attract readers.

Tips for more attention:

1. Several tests have shown that a RED headline is more likely to be noticed than any other font color. The color red is often associated with danger, but it also means, "This is important. Read me!"

2. Remove anything from the page that doesn't support or distracts from the sales message. This includes most animated graphics and intense page background colors that compete with the foreground text. There's nothing wrong with a simple black font on a white background. If you can limit the number of colors used to three or less, this also helps make the document reader-friendly.

3. Do not make the text too wide, otherwise it will become monotonous to read from one line to the next because too many head and eye movements are required.

4. The headline must be catchy and interesting and should immediately catch the reader's eye.

5. The format and layout of the cover letter should be appealing. Appropriate highlighting, bolding, bullets, and subheadings make the letter easy to read.

6. Make the letter very inviting and appealing.

7. The letter should prompt the user to read on. You need to make the prospect read on.

8. Be EXCLUSIVE. If all sales letters in your industry look and read the same, why would a prospect read yours? You can use mascots, humor, cartoons and so on.

9. Focus your message on the reader, not on your company or product. This is a major mistake made by big companies who think everyone should know how great their companies are. But your potential customer is essentially driven by selfish desires. He needs to know what's in it for him.

A QUICK LESSON IN WRITING SALES LETTERS IN A CLEAR MANNER

What kind of sales letter is read? Which type of sales letter promotes sales? Which sales letter keeps the reader interested until the last word?

I would say it has to do with the "chatty tone" of the sales letter. You feel like you're in the home of a good friend who is giving you advice over a refreshing drink and snacks. You are relaxed and feel at ease.

So how do you create a conversational tone?

1) Use concise sentences. When talking to a friend, speak in short sentences. You don't use long, convoluted, difficult sentences filled with jargon.

2) Use descriptive word pictures. Use words that create a picture in your mind. Describe this thoroughly. Create an image.

3) Write what comes from your heart. Do you edit when you talk to your friend? Rarely. Continue to write what comes from your heart.

4) Speak to your potential customer in his own language. Mention something he can relate to and that is not jargon.

Just try it and see the change.

Some tips for better formatting your sales letter

1. The headline should be catchy and located at the top of the page so the reader can read it without scrolling.

2. The best color for the headline is RED.

3. Add your name at the top of the page and before the "sales text" and at the end of the "sales text".

4. Scan and paste your real signature.

5. Use subheadings.

6. Subheadings should be the same color as the main heading, which is RED.

7. Draw attention to your testimonials by inscribing them in separate boxes. You can also use a different color for the boxes.

8. A good testimonial should state exactly what the satisfied customer liked about your product, service, etc. Highlight the specific thing that the person liked.

9. Try not to put the price in red, because red means stop. It may be good for the headline, but not for the price.

10. Bonuses should be related to your offer.

11. Highlight important parts of your cover letter.

12. Use a payment method that has some credibility and acceptance, and even better, offer several different payment methods.

13. Just like on paper, sticky notes on your website capture your visitors' attention for a few seconds. Make those seconds work for you.

14. Use white space to break up the clutter. Give the eye a break.

15. The chosen font and color should be legible and appealing.

16. A sales letter should always include a call to action. Specify how you want your prospect to act. Do not assume that he will already know.

WHICH IS BETTER - A LONG OR A SHORT SALES LETTER?

Does a long sales letter generate more sales than a short one? In fact, long or short is relative. The basic goal is to be interesting. If the sales letter is interesting, then it can sell your product or service, whether it is one page or 24 pages long.
It has been proven that a long, interesting sales letter always converts more prospects into buying customers.

Why is that? A long and interesting sales letter gives the reader the feeling of being with a friend. He awakens a sense of connection that deepens as the letter progresses. He talks to him as if he knows him and cares about him. He creates a bond.

Your letter must identify with your potential customers and try to identify their real needs. The letter should make them feel that you empathize with the reader and recognize their problem.

It should make them feel that you really care about them.

This creates a feeling of trust. The prospect has the feeling that you certainly understand his problems and is eagerly waiting for your solution.

Your letter should be customized for each prospect. Avoid the "mass mentality".
Trust is the most important emotion you need to gain. Once your potential customers trust you, they will not only buy your product or service, but also gladly recommend it to others. Word of mouth is another valuable marketing tool.

So use long, interesting texts for your cover letter.

DO YOU ALWAYS HAVE TO USE CORRECT GERMAN?

Many copywriters believe that they must always use correct spelling and polished German when writing sales letters. However, this is not always the case. Copywriting has very little to do with "proper writing.

Only a small part of the entire writing process involves the "actual writing". It's essentially how you format it and how you present information to your potential customer.

For example: What if I sent you a letter that was typed with an outdated, broken word processing program and contained all kinds of grammatical errors. And the letter would say, "Behind all these typos, I have chosen you in a lottery to send you a million euros as a prize." Do you care about the mistakes and misspellings? No. You are now floating on cloud nine with joy.

On the other hand, assume that I type a perfect letter on the best paper. No spelling or grammatical errors. I also spray some perfume on it. But in the end, I do my best to sell you an old, dilapidated building on the outskirts. Does that interest you now? Oh, no.

It's not how you phrase it, it's what you say.

The bottom line is this: there may be exceptions, but the truth remains that if you focus on distributing your offers with a truly compelling proposition to people who have already shown they are interested in products or services similar to yours, your chances of closing a deal are far higher than if you only target half-interested or uninterested people with a perfectly written sales letter.

A MONSTER OF A SALES LETTER

In most cases, marketers produce their own monsters in their sales letters (just like Dr. Frankenstein).

Sales letters work best when you have something to sell. Basically, it boils down to answers like this: What exactly can you do for me? Why do you think I should spend my valuable time reading one of your letters? Quick ... Convince me that I need the product or service you're offering me.

When creating a better sales letter, start by using the right HEAD, not the wrong head like our Dr. Frankenstein.

The right head can make or break your sales letter. Focus firmly on your target market. Address a big problem facing your target audience (assuming you have the answer). If you can do this through smart wordplay, go for it; however, if wordplay isn't your thing, keep it simple and straightforward. There is no perfect measure of headline length, but don't abuse words. Limit yourself to one sentence.

Once you've captivated readers with your headline, don't let them run away. As we have already seen, the P.S. is one of the most important parts of your letter. So don't waste your P.S. with useless words.

Say something that will encourage your reader to return to the beginning of the letter and continue reading.

The first paragraph is also very important, so get straight to the point. Show them the essence of your offer. Let them know what fortune they will make or how comfortable their life will become or how convenient the offer is and so on.

If you manage to engage the reader through your first paragraph and create interest in him, let the rest of the letter answer the basic questions and address the general concerns your reader may have. Since you worked so hard, it would be a shame to lose him because of technical problems.

Fill the body of your letter with benefits, not just features. Your benefits and features must be able to answer all the "So what?" and "Why you?" questions.

Speak to your target audience in their language. Write informally. Ask questions and answer them. Make the letter as clear and concise as possible. Use humor as much as you like, but make sure it doesn't backfire. Readers should not misunderstand your intentions in any way.

Everyone has a lot of time pressure. But what can you do? You just have to reach readers in the middle. Use bold and highlighting to highlight specific information. This grabs readers' attention and encourages them to read on.

Now you have emphasized over and over again how good your product and services are. But why should people believe you? And what do you do now? Simple. Include some testimonials from satisfied customers. Let them tell your prospects how good your products or services are. Testimonials are an influential sales tool that validates your claims as true.

Once you have cleared up all possible doubts and questions, it's time to put your best foot forward again. Go over your offer. And if you can, offer a performance guarantee. When you offer a guarantee, you reduce the distrust associated with buying your product or service. Consumers are pretty wary, and that's even more true when they're shopping online. And warranties give you almost immediate trustworthiness with potential customers. Guarantees increase perceived value.
When you have finished writing, forget about it for a while. This way you can be more practical when revising your letter.

Before you send out your mailing, test the market. Adjust it according to your response. Then, track the responses to further optimize both the letter and your target audience.

A sales letter will never meet all your expectations. Get on with your other marketing efforts and don't forget to quickly follow up on any leads generated by your sales letter.

Put it together with care and skill. A good sales letter compels your audience to respond positively to you.

Your print shop can help you tactically create a variable print campaign that takes advantage of personalization. In doing so, you need to recognize the value of good printing. That means you should use a good printer and good paper. Even though the actual cost of each mailing is higher, the better return on each mailing at any given time will result in a higher return on investment. The bottom line is that good business printers can help you achieve your revenue growth goals with ease.

Create a reasonable budget. Try to control costs in other ways. But try not to use low-quality paper and poor ink. This will worsen the reader's impression. Basically, it's the content of the sales letter that matters, not the external gloss. Similarly, a good glossy paper and ink will significantly increase the chances of your potential customer reading the letter.

IS IT TRUE THAT GOOD SALES LETTERS ARE LIKE GOOD SALESPEOPLE?

See for yourself. First, compare it to newspaper ads placed for salespeople. The qualities employers look for in salespeople are the same qualities you should look for in a cover letter.

1. Is he a self-starter?

The best salespeople need minimal guidance. They are self-inspired. Similarly, your sales letter must work on its own. If you want your prospect to buy based on the letter, your cover letter must include every benefit, feature, sales promise, proof, and guarantee necessary to close the sale.

2. Does he have previous experience?

The best salespeople learn from their mistakes. So should your sales letters. The letter you plan to send needs to be tested to make sure your list, offer, introduction, and timing are optimal.

3. Can he work well under pressure?

Your prospect is busy and unfocused. Your letter will most likely come across as a disruption. So make sure that your letter captures your prospect's concentration and contains your sales pitch.

4. Does he have excellent communication skills?

Make sure your sales letters are simple and user-friendly. They should speak in the common language of the people.

5. Is he energetic?

Your sales letters must have a distinct liveliness.

6. Does he have proven organizational skills?

A sales letter should be organized and structured.

7. Is he a team player?

Occasionally, your sales letter is not able to work alone. For example, if your cover letter is designed to generate a lead and not a transaction, it will likely need to work with other players, such as print ads, telemarketing, billboards, etc., to achieve the desired goal.

You must make sure that the content of the cover letter is on par with the other marketing tools.

8. Does he have excellent customer service skills?

While it's true that sales letters are a one-way conversation, you can write them to seem more like a two-way conversation, right? The more your letters strike a warm, human and genuine tone, the better.

9. Only serious applicants should apply

Prepare and send a sales letter only if you are serious about offering a promise and keeping it.

10. Like a good salesperson, a good sales letter should always ask closed questions because they allow you to get specific answers and close the sale. Closed questions begin with verbs, for example, "are," "will," "is," "have," "are not," "have not," and "will not." They are answered with a "yes" or "no". You usually use this technique when you want to boost the conversation and get precise answers that will lead you to close the deal.

You can also ask more specific questions, such as "Do you realize you have a problem?", "Will you make this decision in two weeks?", "Do you like my product or service?", "Would you like to start right away?", or "Are you satisfied with your current supplier?". Such questions force the prospect to make a decision.

Always ask closed questions in a caring, friendly and curious tone. Always be well-mannered and friendly. You should never use force or exploitation. It never works. On the contrary, it has a negative effect on your cause. You lose credibility.

THE TEN BASIC RULES FOR WRITING A GOOD SALES LETTER

For many small businesses, a sales letter is their only marketing tool. You may not have the budget for anything else. But a carefully crafted sales letter can have a magical effect on your sales and profits. Just follow some of the guidelines below and you'll see your profits skyrocket.

o **You must always respond to the wants, needs and desires of your potential customers**. Put yourself in the potential customer's shoes before writing a sales letter. Remember, what they are looking for in the letter is, "What exactly is in it for me?" So tell them what's in it for them.

o **Avoid the mentality of the masses. Write to specific people.** Write to a real and live person. Write the letter as if you were writing to a single friend and not to thousands of people.

o **People buy benefits, not features.** You should start by distinguishing benefits from features. The sales letter should be able to persuade the reader to buy your products based on the benefits the product/service provides, not the features. It is the benefit that buyers buy, not just the feature by itself.

o **Captivate your readers with the very first line**. You have to compete with several unsolicited mails at any time. Therefore, your letter should be crisp and catchy. The headline should make the reader read the first line, the first line should make him read the second line, and so on.

o **Provide the reader with specific and relevant information.** Don't go into endless detail about a product or service.

Don't go around in circles. Give specific benefits and tell how the reader's life will be easier because of the benefits offered.

o **Your sales letter must sell**. The basic goal of your sales letter is to sell, right? It has to sell. And to sell, it must be written in an entertaining tone. Speak to your potential customer in a clear and friendly manner. Refrain from using embellished language and consider basic grammar rules optional.

o **Test your cover letter**. Try asking yourself if someone wrote you the same letter, would you be so convinced that you would spend your hard-earned money on it.

o **Make the cover letter as long as necessary**. There is nothing too long or too short. The most important thing is the interest factor. The cover letter should be interesting and appealing.

o **Pay attention to aesthetics**. Use user-friendly fonts and templates that make the document visually appealing. Use bullets and highlighters to increase clarity. Try not to end any page except the last page with a complete sentence. Most newspapers use this tactic. If you don't end the page with a complete sentence, the reader will automatically navigate to the next page to complete it.

○ **Tell the reader exactly what to do.** What should the reader do next? Should he send in a reply card? Or should he place an order? Or call for more information? Make an appointment? Inform him accordingly. Don't assume he already knows. It's amazing how many sales letters fail to inform the reader of the next step. They assume that the reader is a mind reader. But unfortunately, that's not the case.

FIVE USEFUL SECRETS OF AN EFFECTIVE SALES LETTER

The difference between an average sales letter and an effective sales letter is the result it achieves. As explained earlier, it's not too difficult to write a million-dollar sales letter. You just need to follow a few tips and guidelines.

Here are five more insider secrets for writing a "killer" sales letter.

1. Spend a few hours each day going over some of the most effective sales letters ever. Try to learn the finer points. Try to see how they use the headline and how the introductory paragraph is structured. Pay attention to the style, the structure, and so on.

2. You should also collect all the best sales letters you find and create a notebook from them. Then, when you sit down to write a sales letter, you can flip through your notebook of sales letters to get ideas for your project. Do not copy these letters. This would be considered plagiarism. Just take out the basic ideas and put them in your own words.

3. Research your potential targets until you know everything about them. You need to know their wants, their desires, their dreams, and their aspirations. You need to know what motivates them and what doesn't. When you know this, it will be much easier for you to write a sales letter that will have a positive impact on them. Your letters need to be personalized.

4. Learn to relax after you have researched y-our potential customer. Once you have comple-ted your research on the client, forget about it for a day or two. This will allow you to be more practical when composing your letter.

5. There is only one way you can find out whe-ther a sales letter is successful or not. It must be subjected to a test. You need to send it to a number of your potential customers to see if it makes progress

does or does not. If yes, then great, if not, you need to start from scratch again and turn on your mind.

DO EMOTIONALLY CHARGED SALES LETTERS INCREASE SA-LES?

Are you annoyed that your sales letter is not being received properly? Are you at a loss as to how to increase sales with your sales letter?

If the answer to the above questions is af-firmative, then I would suggest that the solu-tion to your dismal results is contained in a sin-gle, but powerful word - emotion. As you may have realized, buying decisions are made based on emotion. The cover letter must build on the reader's feelings and motivate them to act. The letter should attempt to address the "hot buttons" or emotional pressure points that will move the reader to purchase. The two most important motivators are the promise of a win and the fear of loss.

So how can you incorporate more emotion into your sales letters to increase the sellability of your copy? Here are a few examples.

1) Create Ach moments: Try to get inside the reader's head. Focus on the problem the reader is having. Show him that because of this problem, he is stuck, irritated, worried, and unable to meet his real needs. You need to stir up their obvious problem and make it seem worse than it actually is.

2) Attention-grabbing stories: Stories are extremely successful at appealing to emotions. If you see a disaster, you'll feel miserable. If you see a science fiction movie, you will almost certainly sympathize.

If you watch a horror movie, you will be scared. So include stories in your letters that create the expectation of overcoming an obstacle, avoiding difficulty, or achieving a goal. You can also include stories about what happened to someone who didn't try your product to solve their problem. This type of story creates the fear of loss, which is stronger in most people than the desire to

for profit . Tell a story about a person with whom your readers can easily identify.

3) Use emotion, not logic: It's true that some words trigger stronger emotions than others. You should analyze your target market and find out which keywords your prospects actually respond to. The important thing to remember is that almost every single word contains an emotional component. If your offer is profit-oriented, then words and phrases like "money", "get rich quick", "millions of dollars" and "earn from home" will excite your readers. Choose five or six keywords that evoke the desired emotions in the reader and place them skillfully in the sales copy to evoke an emotional response.

As I said earlier, there are countless ways to bring emotion into your cover letter. There are a variety of emotions. You certainly can't put all of those emotions in your sales letter.

Most sales letters target one or two main emotions and then appeal to a few more. The more emotions you can include in your copy, the more persuasive your letter will be.

Your sales letter should methodically explain the benefits of your product or service. At the same time, your product or service should solve a problem that your potential customers have stumbled upon. In reality, every successful sales letter must satisfy a real need.

The right cover letter should build trust from the start and tell a motivating story throughout. This is not a guarantee of an immediate sale, but the beginning of a relationship based on trust.

Of course, you must use emotions morally and judiciously. If you plan to use them, think for a while and ask yourself how you would react if someone else directed that kind of communication at you. This will help you decide how to proceed. Test marketing at every stage is important to writing the "perfect" sales letter.

It may happen that no matter how many sales offers you send out, the effect is zero. Do you know exactly why people don't want to buy your product? Have you ever wondered why your competitors make more sales even though they have a miserable product to offer?

Maybe you feel that people are just not interested in buying your product or service. Or maybe you feel that your price is too high. Or, even worse, you feel that your product or service is useless and decide to quit altogether or perhaps change industries.

This is where you need to stop and think for a while. Is it perhaps not your product? Sometimes it's your own cover letter that turns out to be the main culprit. Perhaps you've unwittingly used certain words that have the opposite effect on your prospect.

So what exactly are the bad or nasty words that you should definitely not use in your sales letter?

1) **Buy.** Never ask people to pull out their wallets and spend their hard-earned euros.

Remember that most people become suspicious as soon as they see this word. No matter what business you are in, using this word can kill y-our business in no time. Instead of using the word "buy", change it to "get" or "invest".

2) **Learning.** This term certainly reminds pe-ople of the old days when they had to learn and study in school. Believe me, no one is interested in racking their brains like they did when they were students. Nowadays, people want quick information and don't have time to learn. It's better to use the word "figure out" instead of "learn".

3) **Say it.** People won't pay attention to you if they can't identify you. Look closely at these two phrases: "I just want to tell you how to lose weight in a week" and "I want to tell you how to lose weight in a week." Which statement do you think will have more impact?

4) **Things.** If you use this word, your sales let-ter will be very boring and uninteresting to read. Instead of the word "things" you should change it to "tips", "tricks" or "techniques". Believe me, this will guarantee a better and more open attitude.

5) **The Stuff.** That's the word most marketers use to explain how great the product is. Compare these two phrases, "Call us for fabulous stuff" and "Call us for fabulous gifts." Which sentence do you think would elicit more responses?

Every sales letter contains a certain vocabulary that is intended to trigger the emotional impulse to buy in you. This language must be used with care.

Look closely; in the sales letters selling you some get-rich-quick ventures, you will come across certain words like "**turnkey**." This means that the business you are to participate in is ready to go and that you will have to do little or no work to make a profit. However, most often this word is used in sales letters to explain software that you still need to install, learn, and operate in order to appreciate the service or product being offered. This is not correct.

Be very aware of the words "**could**" and **"get rich instantly**". You could earn as much as $100 to $1000 per month. Assess what someone who joins your affiliate program usually earns. Do not try to mislead or bluff. Although these words may evoke instant reactions, you must only use them if you mean it. Remember that there is absolutely no shortcut to success. So don't try it.

The success of a sales letter depends mostly on the words you use and how you craft them to serve your purpose. Once again, you don't have to be an expert.

You just need to write simple German in a friendly and conversational tone to write an effective sales letter.

WAYS TO BUILD REPUTATION

Here are some methods to build a good rapport:
• In sales letters, we can often make some statements that are clear yes questions.

For example:
You know how important this is for you, don't you? Don't you deserve the best?
Isn't this the best time to start?
Adding a question mark as opposed to a period is still debatable, so use what you think is best for your situation. Your goal is to get your

prospect to agree with you and do what you say. Play on his feelings.

• Another method, analogous to the above technique, is to include testimonials from satisfied customers. They are very useful to increase the perceived value. But use real testimonials. Do not try to bluff.

Mirroring is another method in which you model your appearance, tone of voice, and jargon on your potential customers who know them well. For example, you won't be talking to a doctor, but to an accountant or event manager.

Reputation is very similar to building credibility. The main difference between conveying credibility and building a bond is that your prospect may trust you, but not be open enough to spend their hard-earned money on your product or service. The fact is that people trust those who are more similar to them than they are to themselves.

Chapter 4 - Completion of the work

FINAL CHECKLIST FOR A SALES LETTER

o It is better to use the name and title of the interested party.

o Try to make the cover letter user-friendly and special.

o Use anecdotes, slogans, and catchy headlines.

o Try to write the way you normally speak. Read your first draft aloud to see if it has a clear and free flow of speech.

o Keep your paragraphs short and use straight-forward language. Speak in the jargon of the target audience.

o When you have finished the letter, forget about it for a while. This will help you be more practical when revising your letter.

o Ask friends and relatives to critique and comment on your sales letters.

o While sticking to a standard format, opt for something eye-catching, such as colorful paper.

o Use a user-friendly font.

o Always use P.S. or P.P.S. to attract attention.

o Use testimonials whenever possible to enhance your credibility.

o Make a genuine and irresistible offer.

o Send out a few reminders.

o Offer a "trade now" option in terms of deadlines, free offers, limited inventory, etc.

o Tell readers what to do next. Don't assume that your potential customers already know exactly.

o Make your cover letter engaging, exciting and appealing.

o Use provocative and catchy slogans, something that attracts.

o Whenever possible, offer a money-back or satisfaction guarantee.

o Include a response card, phone number and/or URL.

o Make it short and sweet, precise and concise.

o If you make your letter bumpy, it is more likely to be opened because it increases the curiosity factor. You can use rubber bands, cotton balls and other spongy things to make the mail bumpy from the inside.

o You can increase readership if you address each envelope by hand. However, check if your budget allows for this. If not, don't overdo it.

o Refrain from adding a company logo to your envelope, as this will worsen the opening ratio.

Companies are constantly looking for ways to improve their marketing results, and this requires a more customized, targeted approach. A well-written and targeted cover letter goes a long way toward increasing your sales value. If you can make the prospect feel like you really empathize with them and genuinely want to solve their problem, then almost the entire battle is already won. You just need to follow a few tips and templates to write a spectacular cover letter that will serve your purpose.

CLOSING WORDS

By now you are familiar with all aspects of designing a good sales letter. Let's just go over a few basic parameters of an effective sales letter.

1. A sales letter must inspire hope to be effective. People today are always under time pressure. Therefore, they are constantly looking for products and services that will make their lives convenient and comfortable. So always inspire hope.

2. Create a sense of urgency. To get people to act, you need to add incentives to the offer. You can create a sense of scarcity by informing your reader that either supplies are limited or that your existing offer is only valid for a limited time.

3. Show yourself as an expert on the subject. If you can do that, your customers are much more likely to buy what you have to sell. Design your sales letter to give the impression that you are just trying to help others and that you are not really profiting from the sale.

4. Pretend to be unbiased when writing your cover letter. People hate being pressured by salespeople to buy. They feel cheated, even if it's really not. So if you can convince them that you just want to help them figure out what they need and how to proceed, your job is almost done. You can expect them to open their wallets to you.

5. Convince your potential customer with fear. This is the strongest emotion you can use to your advantage. Try to get inside the reader's head. Focus on the problem the reader has. Show him that because of this problem he is stuck, irritated, worried and unable to solve his

honest needs to be met. You need to stir up his obvious problem and make it seem better than it really is. Then

tell him how he can get into trouble if he doesn't do something about it. And then show him how your product or service will help him solve the problem.

6. Try to be different. You need to stand out from the crowd. Otherwise, why would anyone buy from you? Perhaps the best way is to tell your prospects not to buy the product or service you are selling them. Yes, this sounds very silly, but it's not. Tell your readers to buy your competitors' products and services. Only if they are not satisfied with their offer, they should try your products or services.

Successful sales letter writing is critical for the owner or entrepreneur of an Internet business. Profits are generated and lost based on sales letter writing. No matter how wonderful your product is, if you fail to convey it to your potential buyers and convince them to buy your product, you won't make it. So learn to articulate the benefits of your products or services.

You don't have to be a great writer to write successful sales letters. All you need to know is how to sell to people. You need to put yourself in your potential buyer's shoes and train yourself to think like them.

Now you know the rules of the game. If you apply these tips and guidelines, your sales letter is sure to have a relaxed and easy reading flow that will keep your prospects reading and ultimately bring you profits.

© Carsten Meinders 2022

1st edition

Contact: Psiana eCom UG/ Berumer Str. 44/ 26844 Jemgum

Cover design: Fenna Larsson

Cover photo: depositphotos.com

www.ingramcontent.com/pod-product-compliance
Lightning Source LLC
Chambersburg PA
CBHW051858130726
47987CB00002B/888